AN ANTHOLOGY OF LOWCOUNTRY POETS
BY FREE VERSE PRESS

WHERE
DESPAIR
RUNS DEEP
& HOPE'S
EMBRACE
WILL KEEP
MY HEAD
ABOVE
WATER.

Print ISBN: 979-8-9871632-6-9

This book was designed by Marcus Amaker using Adobe Express, Adobe Acrobat, and Adobe Indesign.

# PART ONE
we're learning to surface
(poems by student writers navigating identity, emotion, and the glimmers of voice)

# PART TWO

we carry what the water gave us
(poems by adult writers reflecting, reckoning,
and remembering)

# PART ONE

we're learning to surface
(poems by student writers navigating identity,
emotion, and the glimmers of voice)

# Portrait of a Drowning Mind
*by Adyson Hallows*

I am locked in the Universe With thoughts that drown me.
I wonder why my mind is at war
I hear the metronome in the back of my mind,
counting down the seconds
until it's time for the day to begin again, for the waters to recede.
I see light in the distance, a space between, where despair runs
deep & hope's embrace will keep my head above water.
I am locked in the universe
with thoughts that threaten to drown me.
I pretend my lungs aren't constricted
by thoughts that cannot be articulated.
I feel my heart mimic the clock,
whispering deadlines into my ear.
I want to make a difference with the time l have because while
time is limited, my capacity to love is not.
I touch the thin page, pencil lines scarring the paper.
I worry that I will not have enough time
to translate my soul into words.
I cry to the Lord, yearning for a moment of clarity in my endless
cacophony of thoughts, desiring a symphony.
I am locked in the universe
with thoughts that threaten to drown me.
I understand that these thoughts
are blessings, gifts to be unraveled.
I say my true detriment was never time, but fear.
I dream of what the world could be,
visions of what may never be.
I try to be led by hope, not by fear.
My  hope is for the world I dream of, for a harmony to come from
the chaos... To embrace time for the privilege it is.
I am locked in the universe with thoughts that threaten to drown
me, but now I have the key, my thoughts and I are free.

**Heart of the House**
*by Charlee Reed*

Living in a house together
Staying inside forever
Living with you is a dream come true
I love you to

Water dripping from the ceiling
Anxiety has me feeling
Down in the dumps


**Anxiety**
*by Charlee Reed*

Try to hold the pain
when anxiety gets to me
my mom said
You control your brain

even using chains
its hard to not feel dead
you control your brain

Try to hold the pain
every thought
overwhelming my head
i feel like a car going
down a lane

anxiety is still on my brain
the pencil drops the led
this is what happens
when i play the game

try to hold the pain
when anxiety gets to me
my mom said
You control your brain

i believe it i know is true
but sometimes i feel it was you
The people in my head making
me feel dead

## The Shadows
*by Charlee Reed*

In the shadows were woods whispers and creep,
The moon casts spells while the night wind weeps.
Beneath the dark, the shadows dance,
Inviting you to take a chance.
The owls hoots, through the night,
While the moon absorbs your sight.
In this world where the shadows are always playing,
The brave monsters are sleeping and laying.
The shadows could just give a swing,
The shadows always cling.


## Winter or summer
*by Charlee Reed*

when i feel the breeze of air
i feel free without a care
i walk down the road
i wish it snowed
when my brother says
i can't wait for summer
 because winter is a bummer
i disagree i love Christmas
he loves the water
but ice skating is funner
he sees summer i see winter

# bcowetpqkfndrvuwkdpsa
*by mallarilesley*

Have you heard of the Seven Inch Tree?
It's located West in the Cowet.
People there say,
"Once you find it, the person destined to be with you will be
waiting for you."

After years of yearning for Love,
I've decided to set out for the Seven Inch Tree.
The journey is a long and treacherous one,
But Love has to come at a cost.

Of course, I had to know this.
You couldn't go to
the Seven Inch Tree without knowing the costs of Love.
But it has been far too long.
She must be tired of waiting for me.

When I awoke the day of my journey,
Love willed my body to make it a haste one.
So, with Her in mind,
I set out to the Seven Inch Tree.

Upon arrival,
Drenched with filth,
I saw the Seven Inch Tree's shadow.
It loomed in the distance with a powerful presence.
The green leaves raged in the blue sky,
Its roots spread out like arms reaching for my feet,
Beckoning me closer to the heart of the Tree.
. The suns' rays graced it with His warmth.
And in the Great Distance,
I saw Her.
A ball of light.
Hair billowing in the wind,
She, dressed in a white gown soaked with mud.
The one I was destined to be with.

# The Tale of The Seven Inch Tree
*by mallarilesley*

The Woman walked the Earth,
Looking for something to lift the weight of Her responsibilities
off of Her.
On the Seventh day of the Seventh month,
In the Seventeenth year,
She stumbled upon a Sapling.
Just by looking at it,
She could tell it was old and wise.
However,
It was only Seven Inches tall!
Its Small leaves raged with the wind,
Producing a cacophony of sounds.
The Roots hardly graced the surface!

Before The Woman could question it,
The Tree spoke first,
"I do not know why I am so small."
And,
"Yes, I am Seven Hundred years old."
The Woman stared at The Tree,
Looking for an answer.
Her black Hair billowed in the wind.
Her yellow gown shone in harmony to The Sun.
She messed with her Sun dappled brown skin,
Before She answered,
"You are only so young. What is your name?"

The Tree's leaves slowed down,
Producing a more harmonious
and calming sound than before.
"My name is The Seven Inch Tree."
To this,
The Woman handed a response much quicker,
"Your real name."

The Tree went completely still,
Despite the raging wind.
This same raging wind,
That was creating chaos for The Woman's Hair.

"My name is Agape."
Thus,
From then on,
The Woman and The Tree spent everyday together.
The Woman would approach The Tree after She completed her
Duties,
Tending to the Earth and creating Life.
They would talk and talk,
Of their past lives and the future.
They would share jokes,
Often of The Tree and the Plants that bothered It.
The Tree was grateful for Her,
And The Woman, the same.

As time went on,
The Tree began to realize it growing taller,
Towering high above the Plants.
It's Roots spread out like hungry hands,
Grasping for the green of the grass.
Its leaves spanned a total of a mile.
The Woman had to climb The Tree in order to speak to it!
"You've grown so much, Agape"
She said, Her legs draped over Its branch.
"Yes, I have. Thank you."

"What have I done?"
The Woman joked, a smile plastered on Her face.
The Tree's leaves draped across Her shoulders,
Swaying slowly in the raging wind.
"You are the reason why I grew."
The Woman sputtered a laugh.
"Don't be silly."

She leaned on The Tree,
And fell asleep.
The Tree's Branch secured Her spot,
Its leaves providing a soft blanket.
The Tree encased The Woman in a soft cocoon,
Allowing Her to rest.

Thousands of years later,
The Woman was no longer.
She was buried underneath The Tree,
Protected by Its Roots.
The Once-Seven Inch Tree bellowed Its grievances for a while
afterward.
It raged even when the wind was calm.
Its Roots pounced at anyone who came too close.
Too close to Her.

After a while,
The Tree healed.
It became a haven for lovers.
People would seek out The Seven Inch Tree,
Yearning for their lover.
They would arrive at The Tree,
Waiting for the person destined to be with them to show up.
The Tree would offer shelter,
Warming them on the coldest nights.
Providing a listening ear when their doubts clouded them.
It would tell them,
"I once stood here yearning for my lover too. They eventually
come. You just need to wait a bit longer."

## Parents Just Don't Understand
*by Hero Howard*

Some parents cause the death of so many people.
Now let me explain...
Your parents are your caregivers right?
So why do kids still feel pain?
It's not cool, it ain't fair how we get treated like slaves, using us
for their own gain, but then turn around and then buy useless
stuff, it's kind of hard to tell if they even care.
Some parents have gambling problems, drinking problems,
pill popping and spending problems.
Everyday explicit problems, bad with money and
 deficit spending problems especially when a parent
is drunk with a kid then wonder why their child is in the hospital.
Some parents spend a lot of money on useless stuff and forget
that they have a child and
Then turn around and say, "I love you!" No you don't.
Stop with the lies, parents are the reasons why we hear the cries
of so many children.
All of the sighs parents have when they take care of their children
and when kids get bullied or blamed for the way their body is,
some parents don't take accountability then lie and say,
"It's gonna be alright." Why believe them,
they never give us anything to believe in, because they lie about
all of us, they lie about our safety, they lie about our health,
our past, all of this
Profanity, we always hear them on the phone talking about us,
forgetting we have ears.
We need to take a stand because it's getting outta hand.

## Why Men Cry
*by Le'Mar Smalls*

I heard a quote that said,
"Some women looking at you lesser when there's tears on your cheek
but if there's tears tattooed that same girl is a freak."

A twisted rhyme
A bitter truth, it speaks
Of how sensitivity in men is deemed weak

A tear that falls A heart laid bare Met with disdain
A judgment unfair

But ink on skin becomes a permanent stain, It becomes a badge
A symbol to attain.
A manufactured sorrow A curated pain
Wins admiration Again and again

Why is it so?
Why this twisted game?
Where genuine emotion brings only shame. A man's heart breaks
His spirit torn apart
Yet he must hide the tears The ache in his heart.

Is strength then found in the stoic? Silent grief?
In swallowing the pain, Finding no relief?
Must we wear masks?
Our true selves concealed? Lest our humanity be judged

Our stories unraveled?

This is the weight The burden we bear To be strong
Unyielding, to never despair But beneath the surface
A storm may reside
And, sometimes, even mountains crumble and slide

So let the tears fall
Let them cleanse and renew
For in weakness
Our strength shines through
We are not defined by stoicism's hold
But by the courage to let our stories be told

This is why men cry
Though the world may not see
For even in the darkness
We yearn to break free

## Her Beauty in Verse
*by Le'Mar Smalls*

Me, personally, I say she has a beautiful laugh
But in poetry, we say... "A melody of cheer, a sunlit grace,
Dispelling shadows with its warm embrace."

I say she's stunning
But in poetry, we say... "A blush of dawn upon a petal's art,
A masterpiece of nature, stealing every heart."

I say she has the most elegant eyes I have ever seen.
But in poetry, we say... "Twin orbs of wonder, celestial fire,
Reflecting galaxies in their deep desire."

I say she is scintillating
But in poetry, we say... "A vital force, a current swift and free,
A cascade of spirit, wild and endlessly."

I say she is magnificent
But in poetry, we say... "A balm upon the wounded heart's
despair, A whisper of compassion, light beyond compare."

I say she has a heavenly spirit .
But in poetry, we say... "An untamed essence, reaching for the
sky, A symphony of courage, never meant to die."

So though my words may stumble, plain and true, Or soar on
wings of verse, painted anew,
The essence stays, no matter how I try,
She's all these things, beneath the poet's eye.

For whether simple phrase or rhythmic art, The beauty shines,
captured in my heart. And though I strive to find the perfect
rhyme, Her radiance transcends the bounds of time.

**The guilt that fills Y(our) Hearts**
*by Aziia Bailey*

You wiped my tear-stained face
Why can't you see I'm not for you?
I broke your heart again,
yet you still come to comfort
Your touch so gentle, soothing my pain
Yet in your eyes, a flicker of despair
I've broken your heart,
time and time again
But you're here, to comfort and care.

Why do you cling, when I push you away?
Can't you see, my heart is frigid and dead?
I'm a broken vessel, lost in the fray
A wounded soul, forever misled.

You wiped my tears, but they kept on falling,
A constant reminder of the hurt I've caused.
Your love a beacon, but it's also stalling,
A heavy burden, a painful loss.
I wish I could give what you deserve,
A love as pure and true as yours.
But my heart is shattered, beyond repair,
A love so fragile, it can't endure.

I know I shouldn't have done it;
I know I said I wouldn't hurt you again
But my greed engulfed me
Making me go back to my old ways
Throwing me down a painful path of deception
But...I'm truly a liar

The guilt fills the cracks of my heart
It burns and stings, a constant reminder of the pain I caused you
But your heart, pure and unstained

I hate that you don't feel my guilt
I hate that your heart is pure and unstained

I stabbed your heart over and over again,
Watching the scars rive with each slash
Watching your purity drain
Watching your heart dismantle
Maybe I'll fill your purity with my pain and anger
Or maybe....

my nails dig in your unkempt scars
Filling each slash with my guilt
seeping into each deep opening
as it burns and stings
Mixing with the remaining purity you have left
The elegant smell now replaced with burning flesh and hatred

I feast on your purity like a feral animal
feasting on its prey my heart lightens with your purity
While yours is filled with my guilt and hatred
You hate me, right?
You wish you didn't trust me, right?
But...That doesn't matter anymore

You lay on the floor, your body rigid
and ice cold I touched your now pale cheeks
Using my unkempt nails to scratch your cold flesh
You look so beautiful now
So quiet and peaceful
You should have always been like this;
must you have to be so difficult?
I grabbed your bloodied hair and wrapped it around my fingers
"You should have left, now look at you...
this is your fault, darling..."

## Oh baby, my baby
*by Aziia Bailey*


Oh baby, my baby
Your skin is as soft as satin
As smooth as stones

You laughed in my arms
You fell asleep in my arms
Oh, how you cried in my arms
But you threw me away like a broken toy

Oh baby, my baby
Your smile was as bright as heaven
It filled me with such pride and joy
But now only pain and suffering
You moved on now; you smile for someone else
Oh, how envy swallowed me whole and into a pool of wrath

Oh baby, my baby
Why can't you see I'm the perfect fixation for you?
Can't you see he doesn't deserve you?
Can't you see how much you hurt me?

Oh, how it pains me
to shatter this perfect image
I made for myself

Oh Baby, My baby
I made sure that he didn't show up
for our anniversary I made sure he wouldn't ruin our perfect
marriage "He's perfectly fine, darling, I promise"
Yet you wouldn't believe my reassurance Do I not look truthful?
Can you see through my perfect image? You always believed my
white lies
You always believed I was the perfect man What happened?

Oh baby. My baby
Did you see through my perfect image? Is that why you left me?
I couldn't let you go, even if it met hurting another human being
But that wasn't a human being...that was the monster who took
you away from me
I couldn't let him take you away
You said it was your decision, but I know for a fact that it was his
I want you for myself
I want to shield you away from the darkness and hatred... But I
couldn't protect you from myself

Oh Baby, My Baby

I'm sorry, I'm terribly sorry
I watched your red cheeks go hollow I watched your body slump
in my arm
Your beautiful blood stained on my hands I smeared it on my
face like it was paint Like it was my second skin
"My darling now we can be together, forever"

Oh baby, My baby
Our song echoed throughout our house It was as sweet as honey
Your dressed up in your lovely burgundy dress
It makes you as beautiful as the maggots swimming in your cold
torn flesh The ring I gave you still fit even if your fingers are stiff

I styled your hair just the way you liked it even if it looks un-
kempt I swayed your lacerated body gently
Guiding your swollen feet to our song
"Oh baby, my baby, how much I love thee. I promise you I will be
with you forever and ever even if the devil himself is knocking on
our door."

**Oh, Deer**
*by Addison Edwards*

The first time I saw you
I was caught completely by surprise
You did not attempt to disguise any of your intentions
And did I mention
That I was standing naked
In the middle of the road
You rode in a fortress of certainty
Driving a bunker that has wronged you once before
The windows were bolted shut
Duct tape clinging to the front of your fender
Acting as a reminder of the past
As you rolled down your window I asked
How you are able to continue after you have been hurt
"Oh Deer," You sigh as you reach your palm in my direction
"Can't you tell that I'm the one doing the damage?"
And as I began to giggle at your attempt of a joke

You started to laugh at your verbal warning

**The Exterminators**
*by Conner Poss,*
*For my Soul.*


One night, in mid July, the prime of our summer,
They called the exterminators to your house.

For, you– messy, unbridled, addicted, you –
have always hated cleaning.
Resented the way a wet sponge licked the inside of your palm,
Condemned the broom for its shedded shards of hay that lie on
your living room tile,
You would rather live with the mess than simply deal with it.

And I guess, somewhere along the way,
with the dishes piled up,
The clothes married with mildew,
and those sullen, slimy, slinking vermin intruding,
You began to love the mess, to care for it.

Or at least, you got used to it.
You found yourself accustomed to the tunnels,
packed beneath ceiling high obligations
Loving, or rather, obsessing,
over the tipping ticking time bombs of waste.

So, in the heat of the solstice, your mom would climb the moun-
tain of unresolved feelings and hills of trash, to find you–
On bedrest, ailed, drunk and cruel.

It runs in the family – the illness, that pure dependence–
Spotted by the naked eye, identified by the stench of abuse and
repeat genes, Because with you,
there was no stone, nor substance, unturned.

Rooms coated in a layer of turmoil and debris,
40 30 15 11 9 and 4, acclimatized to that unease and anger. Born
into hospital trips and a conformance to hoarding,

Christened in that liquid gold sick.

They didn't really mind at all,
Of course, until the bugs moved in.

It was those little creepy crawlers breeding in your despair,
Uppers and downers nesting in your chest, that began it.

So they dialed the number for the despoilers,
for the exterminators.

For the men in the masks and the women in the gowns, for God
to stop turning his blind eye. "1-800 Get My Kid Clean!"

They invaded the darkness
and woke you from your bed with unease and anger -
Watched while you fought and bit and begged,
groveled and sunk,
While you withdrew—

Leaving claw marks in the pit that was your mattress – though
none of it mattered. You were no match for a cleaning crew.

So they sprayed down the baseboards,
and hosed down the mattresses.
Filed through your journals and snapchat call logs,
Dug into your pants pockets - and purified you.

They crept into your cupboard,
plucked up the tobacco termites,
Collected every pill-bottle-bug,
laid traps for your razor-blade-roaches,
And pointedly poured out your ant-filled bottles of liquor.

They combed through your couch cushions,
Picked out all of the cannabis droppings,
Poisoned the dime-bag-beetles till they skittered away,

And they took you to rehab.
Where they pumped your spotted body full of fluids,
Sent your brain away to group youth therapy, and you called me.

Weeping, snotty and mean, gripping and rueful,
The words came with liters of spit and anguish,
a mouthful of cotton and blood.

Because they sifted through your hiding spots,
until they had abolished any semblance of a pest
- Until there was nothing left of your stashes of oxy insects and
salvia snail trails,

Until they exterminated what made you, you,
And August came.

## Once Upon a Time, You did a Good Deed
*by Conner Poss*

A letter to the sad, old, yellow dog
Who sits outside of the italian restaurant
Drool dribbling, ears rippling
In the wind, matted and marking his scent,

He wears no smile, no wag of his tail.
Presented to him is stringy chicken bones,
A shallow tupperware of water,
And an empty Kroger grocery bag.

You want for nothing more than
The feeling of warm fabric encasing your
Sandy fur, yet when passed by
Outstretched arms you nip and growl–

And even though salvation
May only be two blocks away,
Packaged neatly in a gift-wrapped
Family of four,

Most days, he just prefers the sidewalk,
The stench from the sewer grate, the
Sight of 10,000 men with the same beard and IPA,
And the soft side of a man I once knew,

The man, now sneaking out on break, to coax the mutt
Out of the sun
and into the palm of his hand, where
A pepperoni lies, plucked from the kitchen floor,
Salted and eye-widening – a good deed that

Would surely erase the traces of
Narcissism and the tattoos of abuse,
This now repenting father of 2 can be found
Stroking the dirty mane of an Amici stray while

He dismisses the nips and growls with
Convincing coos of relatability, and the thought of
"Aren't I a great person?"
As they stand—
Canine, defensive and unclean, stationed outside of

The home of bar fights and shirley temples, the
Sidewalk-shelter of broken bottles and dreams,

And my father, kneeling, for the first time in my life—
He expresses their equivalent equipoise,

The hound and you – you and the man, drowned by
Streetlights, sexy posters planted on newspaper booths,
And the hound, grimy blonde, panting, smiling,
Nonconsensually and nonsensically validating your

Self-comfort, because an innocent creature
Can see that you are a good man, bones and all,
Black eyes and felony convictions, anything can be
Absolved in the presence of deli-meat and metanoia.

## Love bubble
*by Abigail Sullivan*

Our shell we worked to build so strong
The bond we have ever growing
You look in my eyes and I look into yours
The light in our souls intertwined like golden strings
We only make each others glow brighter

The bubble won't pop as long as we're together
Your hand brushes mine and my face lights red
As if the thought of you makes my insides smile
Your constant reassurance compresses all my doubts
And suddenly I don't have to wonder

I know
I know where we are
I picture our future together
Like we're anywhere close

But as long as i'm in our bubble it all seems so real

Feelings i've never felt before take the forefront of my mind
Nothing else matters, as long as i'm with you
On our whimsical bubble
Floating into the distance,
Eternally

**Peace**
*by Abigail Sullivan*

I glance across the room
as I feel your presence linger
Every stale memory fading
I'm good at pretending you're invisible
Good at being unattached
My feelings far from gone

Yet masked behind a curtained rail
I'll never understand

you moved your hands from tight around my waist
to another's so easily I want to be at peace
But, Feeling empty
As if you were the only thing filling me
You were filled with a mix
of endless combinations
I was yours
You weren't mine

Longing for the momentary
Though it feels finite
Delirious thoughts and mindsets
Read the writing on the wall
delete the retrospection
Release the regret
And find my peace

It will be a far cry
Unlike my previous
But refreshed
A sharpened version
And whatever that may look like
It will be foolproof.

**swan lake**
*by Keira Grantham*

growing up with the crisp cutting winds of the southern skies
surrounded by the flocks of honking geese
on my grandfather's handpicked land
with peonies blooming in the ash of winter

i watched the angels find their home
in the muck white wings fresh against the dark lagoon

i wanted to be like the swans
pure in the eyes of my homeland

i wanted to glide my feathers against the icy lakes
i wanted to dip the curve of my beak
into the water beneath leave the restricted old farmland
where art and passion are banished never to return again

i wanted to bask in the frost of the tall grass
and i wanted to find my lover
to escape as the ugly duckling and begin as the swan
migrate to the haven where i will bloom

# cat's out of the bag
*by Keira Grantham*

i watched aimlessly
as the matted orange fur
peeked out from the opening
of the glossy black bag

in the driveway of my rusted mobile home
beneath the tire of my stepdad's off white civic
black smoke ripping from the exhaust pipe
and vocal meows filling the volume of the latex shield

the wheel turns
and the car rolls

but behind the roaring engine revs
the machine pops
and the calls turn dull and stifled

the bag's rustling comes to a stop
and i say goodbye for the last time

**Flower Picking.**
*by Cheyenne Hurst*

I love you, I love you not.
When did your smile stop giving me that fuzzy feeling?
I look down at your sleeping face and smile
Though it does not reach my eyes.
I no longer feel an ounce of anything for you

The inky night sky is speckled with the shiniest glitter
The light casts down on you
You look like something from a painting
But I only know how to paint over its beauty
Paint over what makes it so special

The painting looks so different
You are not what I remember looking at from across the class.
I don't know what I'm looking at.
What I see now is something so...not you.
You are not who I love.

My heart empties itself and I stare at the remnants on the carpet.
I look back over at you. Now you just look so...you.
In my eyes you are no longer special.
You don't find me in my dreams
I don't see the special little details
To me, you've lost all identity.
You are just the you from when we first met.

I'm trying to make it work, but the differences are too stark.
I don't ever remember you being like this.
Your voice isn't silky and smooth, it's annoying.
It grates on my ears, chipping away at me.
No, I don't want to goof off during class, this is important.
No, I don't want a hug right now.
I'm going home.
We separate.

We laugh and laugh of how silly we were
A silly little 3 week fling.
Who you were is someone I will always remember
But not necessarily who I want
My heart is like an on and off switch.
I love you, I love you not.


**Pearls**
*by Cheyenne Hurst*


Nets catch little oysters, shucking
Them from the ocean
Into bins and buckets
Clack clack goes the shaken oyster
Pearls bounding against the walls
Of their fertile caves
Deformed and shining
Rolling in skin.
The fisherman opens its mouth,
Harvesting the pearls before throwing
The oyster back in the water
With itchy skin invading the shell
Mouth wide open
The oyster muses on what
Type of jewelry its pearls will make
Earrings, maybe a necklace, even a stud?
Pearls belong in the world
And oysters always come back to the ocean.

**Remaining Legacy**
*by Bri Miller*

remains somehow disappear,
whether ashes or decomposition,
some day I'll disappear

(you will too.)

and all that will remain is my legacy...

a hardcore girl or a weak child still lost?
what will my legacy be?

I do not know.


**the sun and moon kissed once too**
*by Bri Miller*

follow where the river goes,
down the stream to Montage,
Juliet finds Romeo,
in the next life.

With angel wings clipped on his back,
he holds out his hand and says,
"my love, take a chance."

bonnie hikes her dresses high,
clyde rolls down his biker tights,
no bullets take them so soon,
and no car runs, runs, away,
drives by them to the afternoon,
she sings and writes,
he drinks and smokes,
but happy ever afters existed,
somewhere in the biographies of love.

and if the rays of might, moons of lies,
eclipse are faces that touch and pass by,
if they can surpass,
the sweetest loneliest of times,
the sun and moon can kiss once again,
as the sun and moon kissed once too.

**Butterfly**
*by Aniyah Martin*

I love the butterfly

But why can't I fly as high It makes me cry
Every time I try
The weight I feel kills me
As every raindrop-like tear I cry
Rips right through me, I die

But now,
as I go to open my eyes, I'm flying
I don't know how
I'm crying, as I am now,
Ripping right through the clouds I'm finally alive...
With the one I've loved all my life...
Me and my butterfly, can now finally thrive.


**It Leads All**
*by Aniyah Martin*

It bubbles up, then bursts,
A fragile gleam of fleeting light,
Born in a heartbeat, gone in a sigh,
A secret slipping through the air.

It flows unseen, like air,
Slipping through fingers,
Dancing past walls,
Carrying the scent of dreams untold.

It roots itself deeply,
A quiet force in shadowed soil,
Its veins spread wide, unseen,
Drawing life from the silence below.

It branches out,
Reaching for what it cannot touch,
A tangled web of longing,
Binding hearts across the void.

It wears its layers well,
Folds of truth and tender lies,
Peeling back to raw beginnings,
Revealing all, or nothing.

It flips without warning,
A stillness turned to storm,
Chaos shaking steady ground,
Its dance wild, like uncontained lightning.

It blooms in sudden bursts,
A riot of color and light,
Petals soft, yet fleeting,
Its beauty bound to fade.

It runs on forever,
A river with no shore,
Twisting endlessly toward horizons,
Chasing a reflection of itself.

It lasts beyond the fleeting,
Always there, never gone,
A paradox of eternal presence,
Yet never quite in reach.

It feeds on imaginary fruit,
The sweetness of dreams unripe,
Its hunger sated by illusion,
Growing fuller as it consumes.

It hides behind thick glass,
A shadow seen but never held,
Waiting for hands to shatter walls,

For courage to set it free.

It is everything.
It is nothing.
It blooms, it fades, it lives, it aches-
And it will always be.

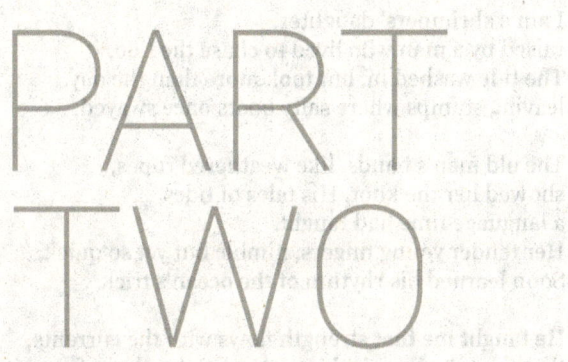

PART
TWO

we carry what the water gave us
(poems by adult writers reflecting, reckoning,
and remembering)

## A Shrimpers Daughter
*by Carrie Parker Ackerman*

In the early light of a coastal morning,
I recall his voice waking me up
at 4am to head out to the docks.

We arrived, and the still, quiet air with melodies from the
seagulls morning whistle and the lapping whispers of salt on
weathered docks, a moment in my memory I shall forever keep
locked.

I am a shrimpers' daughter,
raised by a man who lived to chase the tide,
The tide washed in, but took more than the day,
leaving stumps where salty boots once swayed.

The old man's hands, like weathered ropes,
showed her the knot, His tales of tides,
a language time had taught.
Her tender young fingers, nimble but yet so quick,
Soon learned his rhythm of the ocean's trick.

He taught me that strength flows with the currents,
that the art of survival is written in the glow of sunset  and the
silent promise of tomorrow's pull on the horizon.

Each wave that kisses the bow of the boat
carries echoes of his laughter,
and every stretch of shimmering water recounts the tales  of
nights spent beneath vast, star-scattered skies
As he would sit in his captains chair,
where he sang every word to Alan Jackson
And told his secrets of wisdom born from salt.

She drops his nets in the exact spot he had taught her.
Her muscles strained, a worthy, youthful fight, Hauling the silver

bounty to the light,
From that same stretch
on her first drag he lead,
A legacy of harvest,
richly spoiled with glistening shrimp,
a treasure from the deep blue,
drawn from the spot his knowing spirit knew.

I carry his legacy in the rhythm of my own heartbeat,
in the dreams that sail on the winds of his memory.

Thank you, Daddy, for the love you gave,
and the lessons you taught me,
our  bond so deep, it stretches past the grave.
A daddy's girl I was, and still will always be,

Forever I'll be cherishing your memory,
Don't worry, be happy,
he'll say for heaven is where he'll be.
     He's gone fishing.

## What I Did When I Could Do Nothing
*by Layle Keane Chambers*

red edged    flowed out
to find you
boxed    celled    somehow kept
and I feltuseful

       *of some use to you*

gazed into    tendency
strained and bit
back turned    against the wind
wide open ran

       *but that won't help*

pour the milk    soften
and        swallow, somehow stand
the dust is here, the dish and cup
the dog on the walk

ears up and pressing on
I kneel to pick a goat head
out of love, out of need, out of crying out
what do I do? while you are doing

       *do we need you broken?*

and did I sign up, too?
I don't remember
agreeing to hold my breath
pluck hairs, stare into the blue

       *no, they don't want us grieving*

mother-love immobilized, panic in its place

but the world is unhelped by helplessness, so
gather and bind to us    the air
a letter you sent, favored rock, flattened coin

choke
knowing you won't eat tonight
read    the Geneva Conventions
imagine    surfing

## Becoming a Lighthouse #1
*by Layle Keane Chambers*

cold laps the shore
no choice but to step in
stride out, stake my place
transmute into tower

two minutes since last I looked
no longer 12:59 now 1:01
I count the difference
between my night and your morning
losing you on the Caspian Sea
where signal ends and I
set my clock to wake when
you are expected to land
how should I feel
when you are flying over
Turkmenistan?
I make my feet melt
into bedrock, desire me
into mortar and stone
I strobe the
surface of the earth
I send a beacon
to your soul
should it be jolted free
then you send pictures of the Hindu Kush
mountains I will never see

## Last Seen

*by Layle Keane Chambers*

I saw my son near Bangor ME, near St. John's
near Keflavik and Faroe
climbing a bolted route through clouds
I saw my son body surfing Folly between tides
soaking in the homelight
I saw my son as a green line on a computer screen
    ending at 1:46 am
in the shock of 21 guns
kneeling to offer
packing his bag again
I saw my son crying in the shadow
    of the clocktower
finding the deep water of the stroke
I saw my son near Farranfore, 4:56 UCT
two-fisted, lifting the weight
    of a man who was father to him
I saw my son sipping scotch in a Glasgow pub
twisted in the canal
waving from the porch
I saw him grieve a dream, un-gnarl history
wear an open-heart t-shirt
float a feather in the upstream
in his driveway, in his Jeep
in Tallinn, in Landstuhl
in Rzeszow, in Constanta
on Strada Tudor Vladimirescu
near the Black, Caspian, Baltic Sea
I saw my son nearing Cartwright, Canada
    on this side of the world again
I saw him
check his phone

## Becoming a Lighthouse #3
*by Layle Keane Chambers*

rehearsing, I stand
spinning green lines
and ghost light gestures
at the end of my island
Morris bides
brick and white stripes
no longer alert
the water the light and tides
a pelican formation flyby
the comings and going
shift to cycle
dune grass waves
wait
I am content
to watch
to walk out
to the abutment
sketch my feelings
on sand to show you
someday
when
mission done
white caps wash

**noticed**
*by Heather Rose*

I'm feeling anxious,
because I have so much
on my plate
right now,
that time of the
month
lurks
near,
and
I have a history with
anxiety.

I am here:
the weight of
gravity
pushing me
rooted
to the earth,
heavy,
slowing down
the moment
with my
attention.

breathe
in,
breathe
out.

this moment's
safe.

anxiety
lifts me off the

ground,
helicopter thoughts,
spinning
invisible,
carrying me
away.

it's safe to
land.


**multiplicity.**
*by Heather Rose*


you are an expert
and
there is much to learn

you've come a long way
and
the road ahead is long, and unknown.

you've found your soulmate
and
the work of love has just begun.

you've built your dream home
and
one day you may outgrow it.

you've read the books
and
you still don't know the answers.

you love me as I am
and
hold space for who I might become.

the world is plagued with brokenness
and
painted with beauty.

you are not perfect
and
you are enough.


**it's not the guns**
*by Heather Rose*

they say,
it's the [hurting]
people.

but what if we
took the guns
and gave
support?

we don't have to fear
a person in
distress
with no
destruction.

without the
trigger
we buy
time to heal
the wounds.

**stay**
*by Heather Rose*

just one more
day –

the world is dark,
the pain is heavy,
the future uncertain,
it's true,

but the world,
the future,
(and I)
need you.

you've made mistakes,
I've made some too,
start again and make it new.

close your eyes and feel
the light shining from your core,
burning hot once more.

don't go.
take it slow.

one painful foot in front
another stepping from behind,
believe that this will pass one day,
believe some hearts are kind.

please stay –

don't leave this way.

## The Robin Hood of Horses
*by Kaitlyn Johnson*

Stealing from the rich to give back to the poor

If love was a hoarded resource in this lifetime of war

And I want to know everything about you every little part that makes up your core

I don't care about any darkness that is there now or that ever was before

I'll look at it in its face and give it a roar

Because I have night vision and I'll beg it to see more

Because I know a woman whose bloodline stole from the rich to give back to the poor

And she carries on the bloodline tradition with kindness for me and I
don't know what for

She's as strong as the impressions left in the dust from the gallops of the horses as under thieves they used to soar

And though she will never be more than what a friend is for,
I'll sit cross legged with my head leaned softly against that door

Grateful to be a part of this Robin Hood of horse's lore

# A CAT AT THE END OF A STRING
*by Kaitlyn Johnson*

Did you know trauma can cause your eyes to change color

I wonder if yours has changed over time and if the honey comb
hue is just your current point of view

From time putting its stamp on you

As it sent you through the distribution centers of pain

Without bothering to check the weather reports or delays due to
torrential rain

And I don't know the half of it and I don't know if I ever will

I'll just be happy being a spoke among many that line the
threading of your wheels

As I know they've dug through mud that became quicksand in
the middle of the trail

As the bones that frame your soul could tell

Encasing you like you're a degree in how to be snow capped
mountains that line the sky under a sunset that sinks like its just
as tired as humanity

And I'm drawn to you like a hand on paper

Where I write words of you unraveling me like a ball of yarn

But like a ball of yarn where it has a paw batting the string and
it's exciting as it comes undone

# HOW THEY MAKE US FEEL
*by Kaitlyn Johnson*

Doesn't the saying go that we will forget what people say but we will never forget how they make us feel.

I won't forget either with you, my friend

Because you feel like the days in the past when the sun was a radiant thing rather than a bruised star forced to shine on a clock

Because you feel like the "what we thought it was" of the Mandala effect of life before we realized it was just an illusion covering up the inevitable brutal war of dodging bombs just to survive

Because you feel like the thought of future days that used to bring wonder that now only come and pass because they have to

And I don't know why, and it clings to me like the child on the leg of a parent as they try to leave the room

But I've learned how to feel without BECOMING that feeling.

Without morphing into the personification of the agony of predicted loss

And so, I wade in the feelings as if it were a choppy ocean that leaves behind the taste of its salt but also that's just a part of the ocean

And who doesn't want to go to the ocean

And you feel like the love that exudes between you and your wife

And if at the end of the day the only thing that exists good, is you being loved how you should

Then it's all alright by me and occasionally I fear a little less the gnashing noise of the city

And it's a cruel border that lies so out of reach that you exist as if you are my favorite character in a book in a magical realm. And the book can only ever sit on the shelf

But I take it off and read a page each day

And each page feels like the color that used to stain the glass before time eroded the hue from the window and just left the pain

And I don't know why but I don't fight it or try to add to it. I just let it be and have its autonomy

Because we will forget what people say but we will never forget how they make us feel, right?

# Bless
*by Linda Joy Walder*

The dreams
they wake you up
from dreary days in bed
when it's an effort to sip water
or eat a crust of bread

The changes
they unfold in chapters
becoming stories
you tell
but no longer
can rely upon for accuracy

The realizations
they happen gradually
then suddenly
fall from the clouds
raining lightly and fiercely
on your flesh

The peace
letting all things be
to fly or die
observing how they come and go
while you stay whole
is how you bless your soul

**Ode**
*by Linda Joy Walder*

Oh South Carolina beach
as far as my lonely heart can reach
into the ocean of days
that float away in blue.

Oh South Carolina coast
resurrect me from the ghost
I have become in morning light
and hug me near to you
throughout the dreadful night.

Oh South Carolina tide
I will follow as you abide
on windy seas so briskly torn
on balmy crests sunlight adorned.

Oh South Carolina sea
I ride you gingerly
into a balmy peace
from sorrow's savage lease

**Thought**
*by Linda Joy Walder*

Today I had a thought,
What if I never met you?
Would you have existed
in my mind as sunshine behind clouds?
Or, would I have remained alone
under tree branches
blocked?
Would I have appreciated the gentle majesty of the sunrise
and the heaviness of the dark night
if I had not loved you
if I had not tried?

# When Katie Left
*by Linda Joy Walder*

By the time Katie left
I realized how far away
I had been
only knowing what I thought
I knew about her
but knowing nothing of who she was

I had formed an opinion about Katie
long ago
based on minor interactions
at book group and canasta games
but truly I knew nothing about her
even though she lived across the street

As she was dying
I saw her sometimes
walking slowly on the sidewalk
in front of her house
holding her husband's arm
to steady her,
I thought she was very brave
but I did not know her

Until this morning,
when randomly I was looking
at pictures on my Instagram
and I noticed she had liked one of mine,
the one when I had covered our front gate
with balloons after my husband
finished chemotherapy,
I had no idea she cared

Then I looked at her pictures of
family beach days

grandchildren
dogs and flowers
how soft she was
I had not known

And my tears
rolled down my cheeks
because we were so much alike
but I hardly knew her
until she was gone

**Palestine**
*by Natasha Akery*

You're forced to decide
If you will remain at home
Or watch it explode

Pillars of fire,
Smoke and cloud -
Children paint

The war pauses
Women sit in rubble,
Their babies smile

From the womb's white noise
To the whistle of missiles -
A silent newborn

A woman wails
Her daughter's name,
Caked with gray dust

Your loved ones
Under white sheets
In battered streets

The flour
Is wet
And red

Golden hour -
The upturned faces
Of child martyrs

Jigsaw puzzles -
They gather the pieces
Of their loved ones

Dawn on your face
The sun knows your rage
But listen - a wren

## Halmang
*by Natasha Akery*

great grandmother
the bark of her face
reflects the rings of age
her white blouse, crisp
her purple skirt, pressed
your prayers tucked
in layers in her pockets
she closes her eyes
she sees your face
in the land of the dead
she lives because
you won't forget

## Algorithm
*by Natasha Akery*

Do you prefer a quiet war
with silent casualties -
ghosts that stay inside their graves
while unseen mourners grieve?

Do you prefer a mute lament
expressed behind the scenes -
smiles painted on our faces,
cloaking muffled screams?

Do you prefer to turn your head
as neighbors cry for help -
Or will you pause and see in us

reflections of yourself?

# SELF-PORTRAIT AT 25
*by Faith Walker*

The body of her is so desirable:
the curves of breasts, buttocks, hips.
Her heart does not beat for these strange men -
what would they do with the birds in her head,
the blood that is hers and her mother's
and her mother's and and and —
They will overlook the tenseness of her -
she is some kind of bookish kink to be enjoyed.
They imagine her falling into bed,
but they don't see how she gets out -
the wild prayers to makeshift alters,
stuffing back the cracking of her heart,
stuffing back the pain behind her eye,
bolting out of bed at the last second
because the fear of failure has been proven to her before.

He puts his hand on the small of her back
 (he looks so much like) - this man she does not know,
tells her that he needs (the first man to take)
helpprintingabooktolethergofirstbecausehessuchagentlemanand-
besideshelovesthewaysshewalks
and she behaves like a Good Girl does (what she did not give):
she laughs at his unfunny jokes, and smiles.

At home, she stands, silent, stripped,
in front of the mirror.
The pulse in her veins is beating, beating, beating -
even it will not do what she wants and stop.

### We first spoke of summer
*by Sofie Williams*

We first spoke of summer
A clouded far off haze
Of a dream of a place
Sunbeams hitting the backs of our necks
Warming our skin
And raising the corners of our mouths just a smidge
With water lapping at our toes
Half buried Splashing about

### No longer the raging storm
*by Sofie Williams*

When we spoke of summer
Constellations out of thoughts
We strung together galaxies
Of what would be.
Toiling over castles-
Perfectly constructed-
And a view like no other

And at once summer
A collision of plans and unplanned to-dos
A mess
Of convoluted greatness
We built and unbuilt tower after tower after turret
And planted the seeds of a literary harvest

And what bespoke of summer
I never thought you would leave
The tide rolling in
And swimming out
We feel it in the breeze
As the usual birds flap their rounds
Around the marsh
Echoes of an enchanting summer song

**Eve of Icarus**
*by Sofie Williams*

I faked my death
At least, I forestalled it
I had to get away
And I already knew how to fly

Never on land was a thing so important
Never a landing
That I thought to impress
Flying low can sink a man
As much as sun will melt the glue
Feather falling every second

If you're up there,
Don't shove the sun
Out of place
You'll only get burned
And don't forget your flare

An accident of wind
Or faulty fixtures
Or ill prepared pursuits
Perplex and permeate

The good of mankind
I, being so wrought in fear,
Am trying to be good
Wash myself back

Instill a purpose clear within
The waves waiting in their always dance
Balance falls back
A knife's edge
Plunged in darkness

Our names in light
Our bodies stand before us
Uncompromising plights
How strange

**What is your cycle?**
*By DaJenqiue McBee aka @Speak_nek*

Everybody got eyes
Yet they still can't see
Not this natural realm
I'm talking spiritually

Can't seem to figure out they're in a cycle
With their eyes closed
"I do what I want" and "I go wherever I go"
Free will went to your head and got your mind gone

And yet they can't even shake the demons
because their eyes are closed
You got a problem but won't go to the source,
for the answer

Day after day
still stuck in the same matrix
going the same direction

The enemy wants you off course
to stop your progression
Stunt your elevation
Get you away from what
God had already predestined
and get you out of place

Don't let it be a distraction
Be aware on what's really happening
We're not here to be cute or follow the trends
We're here to do God's work and let his light shine from within

So I gotta few questions..
What cycle are you in?
What has you in the same place or moving backwards?

What has you bound and feeling stagnant?
What's your distraction? Why can't you seem to move?
What has you stuck and feeling confused?

Sit down with God
And let him minister to you
Let him lead you on what you should do
Because he is all knowing and omnipresent
And he'll tell you the answer if you let him

You won't have to second guess
He'll give you wisdom, knowledge and understanding,
if you let him
And I know we all have questions
But that shouldn't stop or hinder
Where we need to be
when that call come thru you better answer

## Vessel
*By DaJenqiue McBee aka @Speak_nek*

My body is a vessel like a vast that covers my soul
My mind, will and emotions all wrapped up in one
To be a walking testimony
and to tell all that God has done
He hears my cry, he even knows my pain
I just have to be willing to allow him access to all that I proclaim

He fills me up when I'm low
He restores what has been broken
He is the rock on which i stand
He is my God, the one the only

When I'm in my worship I'm filled with his love
I can share my brokenness to the sky up of above
And the best part is,

he hears me
When I'm feeling weak
When I'm feeling empty
I am his open vessel
And he's my Abba, father

He loves me as me
He cares because I'm his daughter
I've been broken and I've been scarred
But his love mends all of my heart
And he teaches me how to be a light in the dark

I'm his open vessel
And this is my love letter
To my Abba, Father up in a Heaven


**Rewired**
*By DaJenqiue McBee aka @Speak_nek*

When the mind is made new in Jesus Christ
It will change your life
Everything has to change

And it's a steady process

A promise he said he will make right
To be made over and transformed
To be exactly who you are
Before someone made you feel a way
Before the lies and manipulation
Before the hurt or the pain
To be exact who you were made to be

A beacon of light, his wonderful masterpiece
God will take that same hurt and turn it around for you

He'll show you your boundaries
and how far you can go
Sometimes it's a no
because you can get tempted and lose your soul

You have to be willing to have a new way of thinking
You can't bring the past into the things he changing
It's completely new

You are new and as you learn Gods character
and the love he has for you
You will grow trust and build your faith

**Four Poems**
*by William Lawrence Johnson*

I.

it feels a lot like this

melancholy
as relentlessly soaking rain

helpless
as nestlings shaken from the brood

wistful
as the plaintive cooing of doves

hollow
as the roll of distant thunder

until the lightning strikes

II.

sound the applause
as players bow
to vicissitudes
among the stars

taking leave of a stage
where once reigned
what might have been
rains now
a shower of sundered script

proud deportment
exiting left

kicks promise to perfidy
doubly crossing to a more alluring set
surrendering the vanity of dreams
to a more conventional
more scripted

reality

leaving

the downtrodden
shredding this farewell note
a lovelorn testament
to the folly
of heedless romance

sowing now
its fleeting fancy
among wisps of nostalgia
scurrying underfoot
stepping now
into darkness upstaged

confetti dreams

leaping to the shuffle
of leaden feet
showering lamentation
in their wake


III.

(to brother Thomas Wolfe and the homes that elude us)

Tom, you tell me:

Did I die in New York
when fire and fury
spewed smoke and glass?

Or was it
in seventy-three—
when my face
flushed red under the glare
of neon
burned fierce at the wink of a woman
who brazenly offered satisfaction
cheap—
as I strolled the sidewalks
of forty-second street?

An abyss divides them now,
rending their before and after—
pedestrian days
taking wing with malevolence

dashed interred
all
fall
down

Still I recall
near century's end
midtown

the wrecker's ball

creeping west past eighth avenue
razing buildings
that had fallen
first
into disrepair
and later

into disrepute

storied walls
on the lone remnant of which
Adult Books
suspended mid air and time
presumably giving way
that decadence might rise toward new luster

that wrecker's ball

alas
moved too slowly for some

And so . . .

subsequently
downtown
malice deigned to drop majesty
to rubble

And so . . .

even today
on my refrigerator door
a jagged skyline serves to remind me
that twins once towered behind the magnets—
a faded photograph roughly torn
the work of unsteady hands
trying to get a feel for
the magnitude of disaster—
a palpable rift
no camera's eye could capture
anguish
configured along an uneven edge
that traces an arc beyond our imagining
where the flash of death

slashed a hole in the sky

Oh, Tom . . .

fellow exile:
Is it even worse than we first imagined?

How can we expect to find home again
now that these rough streets
having already closed the door to Eden
look for all the world like hell?

There was always the sky,
wasn't there, Tom?

That milky way—
broad and bright—
sustaining us from afar
and beckoning our return.

But now . . .

have the stars themselves gone out?
Like you and I—
fictions unraveled
when silver darts sliced september sky.


IV.

love that's it isn't it
but hardly vapid sentiment
no you you weigh on me
the pull of gravity drawing me
ever deeper into myself
and in the depths of myself
into union with you

yes you you who withhold
vast unspeakable mystery
gravity's own bending
that vacuous field of emptiness
that 'til now
I took for my lot
destiny's portion
to be borne alone

# a note ...

i've always believed poetry is how we breathe when the world tightens around us—how we build bridges between strangers, and sometimes even back to ourselves.

the title of this anthology comes from a student's line—one that stayed with me long after i read it. it reminded me why we do this: to reach toward something tender and real. something that might keep our heads above water.

thank you to every poet who trusted their words with me. and to every reader who enters this book with an open heart. i hope you find yourself in here.

Marcus Amaker

*Dad + Husband*
*Charleston, SC's first Poet Laureate*
*SC Literary Hall of Fame inductee*